Shamanic Soul Retrieval

"Lisa Biritz presents a clear and simple way to use the concepts of shamanic soul retrieval on one's own for resolving many personal problems. Anyone, even shamanic practitioners, can gain from what she offers."

Me ke aloha,
Serge

Serge Kahili King, PhD, author of *Urban Shaman* and *Dreaming Techniques*
Huna International (huna.org)

Shamanic Soul Retrieval

Calling Back Lost Parts of the Self

Lisa Biritz

EARTHDANCER

AN INNER TRADITIONS IMPRINT

DISCLAIMER The author and publishers accept no liability for the methods and exercises described in this book. Neither the author nor the publishers shall be liable for any damages that may arise from using the tips and advice set out in the book. Consult your doctor or alternative practitioner in the event of any health concerns. The methods described do not represent an alternative to therapeutic or medicinal treatment.

First edition 2026
Shamanic Soul Retrieval
Calling Back Lost Parts of the Self
Lisa Biritz

Editing by JMS books LLP (www.jmseditorial.com)

Originally published in German as *Seelen-Medizin, Mit schamanischem Wissen und Seelenrückholung zu innerer Ganzheit*

Cover design: Design Is Identity
Cover illustration: Chizhevskaya Ekaterina/shutterstock.com
Layout by Silja Bernspitz & Janina Vogel, Schirner
Typesetting: Chris Bell, cbdesign
Typeset in Hypatia Sans Pro

Printed and bound in China by Reliance Printing Co., Ltd.

Cataloging-in-Publication Data for this title is available from the Library of Congress.

ISBN 979-8-88850-402-4 (print)
ISBN 979-8-88850-403-1 (e-Book)

Published by Earthdancer, an imprint of Inner Traditions
www.earthdancerbooks.com, www.innertraditions.com

For Steven

Contents

Foreword by Susanne Hühn and Mike Köhler **9**

Introduction **12**

What Is Shamanic Soul Retrieval? **17**

The soul: a luminous sphere of light 18

Exercise: The healing work of the glowing "soul sphere" 21

Soul retrieval with children 24

What Exactly Is Shamanism? **30**

Shamanism exists everywhere 30

Shamanic techniques 31

Shamanism, supported by the World Health Organization (WHO) 37

New Western shamanism 40

Exercise: A journey into the soul world 44

Why Do Soul Parts Leave? **46**

Microtrauma in everyday life 47

Pregnancy and birth 48

Exercise: Relive your journey to life 50

Childhood 52

Entangled lives and dependencies 54

Exercise: Becoming free in relationships 60

Trauma, coma, and death 62

Past lives and collective themes 67

The symptoms of missing soul parts 70

Exercise: Dismemberment 73

Healing **75**
Exercise: Self-healing 77
How do soul parts come back to us? 78
Exercise: Soul retrieval 82
Time for action 84

Maintaining Vitality: Care of the Soul **87**
Integrating soul parts 87
Exercise: Soul part integration 88
The characteristics of a healthy and complete soul 90
You are whole when you feel whole 92
Exercise: A journey into your inner garden 93

Health from the Shamanic Perspective **94**
Illness: too little or too much 95
Intruders and possessions 96
Exercise: Cleansing foreign energies 101

Soul Retrieval for the Earth **104**
Soul loss in nature and the Earth 105
Exercise: Soul retrieval for the Earth 108

Acknowledgements **110**
Bibliography **111**
Picture credits **111**
About the author **112**

Foreword

By Susanne Hühn and Mike Köhler

Susanne: Shamanic work, soul retrievals . . . it all sounds rather complicated, conjuring up images of strange rituals and elaborate trance journeys. But there's something about this subject that fascinates us, Mike and me. And so we travel to Vienna and sit in a circle with Lisa Biritz and all those wanting to discover Core Shamanism for themselves. We hold a drum in our hands for the first time. It feels good, familiar, and yet also exciting and new.

I've been doing psychological and spiritual work for a long time and feel at home with soul retrievals, but what Lisa conveys is so clear and logical, and so powerful, that it revolutionized my entire work. Suddenly I do not have to do everything all on my own! There are power animals, helper animals that go on journeys for me; there are forces at work that I had previously only expected to find among indigenous peoples or in the deepest Amazon jungle.

Lisa is gifted in making these energies accessible in such an easy and natural way that it feels like coming home.

Mike: Lisa dispelled all my remaining reservations about shamanism with ease. I had always suspected that something important was waiting for me, and through Lisa I discovered my own approach.

Since she explains everything so clearly and without fuss, but without any hint of superficiality, it was very easy for me to put into practice what we had learned. Her classes are characterized by great awareness and a sense of responsibility, yet at the same time are conveyed with such simplicity that anyone who is interested in shamanism can only gain from them.

Susanne: So it is possible for a book to convey the really "strong medicine" of soul retrieval? Yes, because in truth it is totally natural.

Lisa writes: "Shamanism teaches people that communicating with the source of everything that exists—the Divine—is a natural part of life. With the right techniques, everyone can learn to see the invisible world and communicate with it."

And that's exactly how it is. It does not necessarily require complicated techniques or deep trance journeys. Lisa teaches us to connect with what we have always known deep inside.

We are a part of the great, all-embracing creator soul, and we may see ourselves as such. Soul work is not the exclusive domain of just a few. Thanks to this book, everyone who can and wants to deal with energies mindfully and responsibly will have the tools to perform great service to themselves on their path to wholeness.

In her simple, direct way, Lisa describes what a soul is and how parts of it can be lost, using simple images that everyone can visualize and understand and which are therefore full of power.

Mike and I are extremely grateful to Lisa for having made the path to shamanism so easy for us and for showing us just how natural and connected to the Earth this path is. We value you very much as our teacher, dear Lisa, and we hope with all our heart that this book will reach many people so that our world can become much more healed—we all hold it in our hands.

Susanne Hühn and Mike Köhler

Susanne Hühn and Mike Köhler are spiritual and shamanic teachers and authors.

Introduction

The majority of people who consult my practice have already sought advice for their health concerns from many doctors. However, conventional medicine has only been partly able to help them. Their symptoms would often be alleviated for a short time, but would reappear in exactly the same or in a similar way at a later stage.

In the process of searching for healing, the path to a shamanic practice is deeply rooted in the history of humankind: medicine men and shamans, similar to our doctors and psychologists, have long worked together in ancient indigenous cultures. They were frequently even the same person, with the one complementing the other, together in the healing process.

It is therefore only natural that sooner or later many people turn from conventional academic medicine to alternative healing.

My clients are entirely justified in seeking a complete healing for their physical or psychological concerns, sensing intuitively that the deeper causes and solutions may be found in their soul.

Like almost everyone practicing shamanism in our Western world, I too found the path to ancient healing methods through my own health issues and a near-death experience. Shamanism even has a specific expression to describe this—a wounded healer, someone who, due to a life-threatening illness, a psychosis, or a near-death experience "goes to the other side" and returns to life of their own accord. They bring with them knowledge and an understanding of the path to recovery on a deep cellular level. Consequently, they are well placed to accompany other people in their healing, and at the same time develop a compassionate heart for all beings, something that is a prerequisite for good healing work.

Although my childhood was characterized by affluence, I grew up nonetheless in a strict parental home and was raised in accordance with what might be termed old-school ways, as did many of my generation. My parents were shaped by the Second World War and the postwar era. For them, their expression of love was that we children should grow up with material security, leaving little room for feelings, which were rationalized or suppressed.

In addition, as I emerged from puberty into adulthood, I had to watch helplessly as my brother—and this is how I explain it to myself today—slipped into schizophrenia due to birth trauma through lack of oxygen combined with our harsh upbringing. To witness how a person whom I loved dearly could lose his mind and his grounding and suffer deeply as a result was one of the most painful experiences in my life, characterized by feelings of total powerlessness.

I myself suffered from problems caused by a slipped disc and pains in the lower abdomen during that time. Not surprisingly, I was also psychologically imbalanced, my emotions fluctuating between fear and anger. It often felt as though my soul were burning. Everything hurt and my heart was crying out. I was not free and I was not happy.

The many doctors that I consulted could help me only superficially or not at all. To some extent, my conditions

even got worse. I was groping in the dark and had no idea why I was feeling that way. I realized I had to consciously seek out becoming healthy. Since I found no answers in the West, I traveled around the world to seek teachers on every continent. It was my only chance to become healthy and happy again. During this time, I also went through a near-death experience in Asia, during a short but very severe and dangerous illness.

I tried out pretty much everything during my fascinating travels, from yoga and shiatsu, via faith healers and gurus in India, to the shamans of North and South America and African and Australian healers. I spent time with those who really helped me and received their training.

Shamanic soul retrieval is one of the methods that helped me, and in a surprisingly simple and yet such effective way. It is worth noting that it is practiced by all indigenous cultures, regardless of where they are in the world. It is performed, for instance, by the Aborigines, the indigenous peoples of South and North America, and the ancient Mongolian peoples. This is because the understanding of life energy and vitality as an intact, shining, and vital soul is universal, as are the methods of making the soul whole again when it has been harmed or injured.

During my travels, I have learned that healing is essentially very straightforward. You just need the appropriate tools.

With this book, I want to give you a guide to understanding soul retrieval and making the soul whole again. I also recommend my oracle card set entitled "Soul-Medicine." This will help you to rediscover your soul fragments so that you can shine again, wake up with joy in the morning, and enjoy life to the full with a spirit of adventure.

Although the exercises described here are very effective, you may not be able to make progress with some issues. In which case, please seek help in the form of a professionally conducted soul retrieval with a trained and practicing shaman.

However, to use the exercises in this book, no special training or specific skills are required. The invisible world opens up to anyone who is sincere in their search for healing, wholeness, and truth. You will soon be able to feel and enjoy your vital, radiant, and healthy soul again.

You are whole when you feel whole!

Lisa Biritz

What Is Shamanic Soul Retrieval?

We are all familiar with the phenomenon. Some people are just bursting with vitality and seem to be ageless, although they may already be way past retirement age. But it has nothing to do with plastic surgery because their lives are clearly visible in the lines on their faces. These people often seem to have more energy than some of their younger contemporaries who could be their grandchildren. Looking at them, you might think in admiration that you would also like to age in the same way.

Where does this energy and vitality, independent of age, come from? Where does our life force come from in the first place?

As is often the case, the answer is so obvious and simple that we readily overlook it—it is the soul that contains our life energy. Like a glowing, luminous ball of light, it gives us vitality. In Hawaiian huna shamanism, for example, the soul is even described as a "bowl of light and life."

The soul: a luminous sphere of light

When I perform healing work, I ask my clients to imagine their soul as a vibrating, glowing ball of energy. As soon as they close their eyes, they can nearly always see their soul sphere clearly, and also see where parts are missing.

Over time, due to painful and traumatic experiences, fragments of our soul energy may leave us. In modern psychology this phenomenon is known as **dissociation**, and in shamanism **soul loss**. When there is no possibility of changing or healing a painful experience, parts of the soul split off and leave. This act of leaving and finding a safe place where fragments of the soul can no longer be hurt is often the only strategy that we humans have left to protect ourselves. At the same time all memories of the painful event follow the soul fragments, which is why traumatized people frequently cannot remember stressful events at all.

When fragments of the soul are missing, we feel dull, incomplete, and lacking in essential life energy. The consequences can range from constant fatigue, depression, chronic illness, addiction, and recurring accidents to personality disorders. We feel as though we are not really living but are functioning on "automatic pilot" or as if we are living our lives for something or somebody else. These fragments of the soul do not return on their own.

Where do these soul fragments go? They consist of energy and so continue to exist since energy is never lost; physics

teaches us this too. These missing soul parts can be very close to us, often even still within our energy field, but they can also hide or go astray in remote areas of the Earth or the galaxy, or even in parallel universes.

In the shamanic world view, everything is connected with everything else, all is one. This interconnectedness is also confirmed by quantum physics, which talks about the "quantum field" and "quantum waves." This is why it is possible to bring back to our soul those fragments that have splintered off, along with their associated characteristics.

But how do we do this? How do we bring back soul fragments? How can we guide our soul back to its full vibrancy once more? The answer is with shamanic soul work and its tens of thousands of years of traditional practice. Soul retrieval fills the "hole in our soul" so that our life force can return and we may be joyful about life again.

The information presented in this book is based on Core Shamanism. This type of shamanic work has been supported by the World Health Organization (WHO) since 1980 as being just as effective in the treatment of psychosomatic problems as psychotherapy, and likewise in maintaining a healthy balance of the four aspects of being human: body, mind, emotions, soul.

Exercise

The healing work of the glowing "soul sphere"

Begin by making yourself comfortable, sit down and relax. Close your eyes and take your time to calm and settle yourself. In your mind's eye, visualize your soul as a shining ball of light.

Take the time to observe it closely. What color is it? Perhaps more than one color? Is it glowing or pulsating? Is it complete or are parts missing? Do you see splinters, nails, or dark spots? You might also receive inner images or insights into how these holes in your soul were created or from where the wounds originated.

Now imagine a wide, cleansing beam of light permeating you, suffusing your body and your soul from top to bottom. This powerful beam of light flows up through you out of the magma of the inner Earth, flooding up into the endlessness of the universe. It cleanses you of all old energies, past injuries in your cellular memory, and external influences—energies that do not originate from you but that have been deposited in you.

Its color brings feelings of well-being: crystal white, glowing red, a rainbow of color, whatever healing colors may show themselves to you.

Allow this stream of light to flow through you for as long as you like.

Now visualize a bright ray of pink light streaming down from the stars and the sky like a gentle spring rain. It carries with it parts of your soul essence, soul fragments that are ready to return to you.

Feel how these parts of your life energy, your vitality, flow down through your crown to permeate you. Feel how you become warm inside, how you relax and feel good.

Allow it to suffuse you with light for as long as you like.

Now notice how much the glowing sphere of your soul has changed. When you are ready, open your eyes once more.

Suggestion

Make a painting or drawing of your soul sphere as you see it now. There is no need to spend a long time on this, the image does not need to be beautiful or perfect. What is important is that you depict what you perceived.

This exercise can be repeated many times, visualizing and then drawing your soul in your efforts to make it whole. Healing the soul is often a prolonged process, but with the aid of such images it can be successfully achieved and documented.

Soul retrieval with children

Since work with the soul can be expressed well visually, it can be performed easily, not just with adults but with children too. Children immediately understand what I mean when I ask them to describe or paint their soul sphere because they are still so close to the mystery and wonder of life. Why we and the universe exist is a profound mystery that no human will ever understand. I have never worked with a child who did not grasp or understand the process of soul retrieval.

Children nearly always greet the idea with enthusiasm, often to the astonishment of their parents, who may have already sought advice for their little ones among doctors, psychologists, and healers. This is why the children who come to my practice are sometimes already anxious, irritated, or bored.

As soon as I ask them to visualize their soul as a luminous ball of light, however, they look at me with interest, and when asked to draw their soul sphere, they all take part. When we perform the soul retrieval ritual, using burning sage and invoking spiritual forces, everyone is fully involved in the process.

Children love the feathers that I use for soul retrieval, all the shells, stones, and other ceremonial objects. Most of them want to touch and hold them in their hands, which I happily allow them to do. These objects are not what enables the healing to happen, they are symbols for the forces and energies that are at work invisibly. They enable us to visualize the ceremony and the healing work, and to make it comprehensible to children and of course to adults too.

Children love ceremonies, such as at Christmas and the ritual of going to bed every evening, which is why they have a natural understanding of the soul retrieval ritual. Ceremonies nourish the soul. They provide security and create a protected space in which something takes place, a change, a transition, something new . . . and healing.

Nothing touches me more than working with children. Sometimes I cry with them as well, out of compassion, especially when working with the wounded soul of a child. When a child suffers, my heart aches with empathy and love. I imagine that everyone is familiar with this feeling, along with the wish that all the children of this world could be well and happy.

A woman comes to me with her ten-year-old son. He is troubled by nightmares and is afraid to fall asleep, and so is constantly tired and nervous.

I use the ball of light image to explain to him how soul retrieval works. He understands it well. I ask him to draw a picture of his soul energy. As he does so, I see that large parts of the light are missing. I ask him where he thinks they are. He says he does not know. I ask him if he would like to try and find out and maybe get them back. He says yes.

During the soul retrieval work, as I guide him into a trance, he tells me he sees his father and mother. They are fighting. His parents separated when he was two years old.

He tells me he is sleeping and then wakes up in his cot. His parents are shouting, his mother is also crying. Then he hears his father making his way to the front door with heavy footsteps, slamming it shut, and leaving.

The boy says that he leaves with his father. I ask him if he goes with him physically. He says no, but his light soul energy leaves, going out of the boy's bedroom and away from the house, following his father. It is still with him.

I make contact with this soul part of the boy and ask if it wants to come back into him, where it belongs. It says no, it wants to stay with the father.

I ask what it needs to come back home, into the boy. It says that the father should promise never to leave him again.

In the trance, I let the boy talk to his father and ask him never to leave again. The father answers, "But I never left you! I had to leave your mother, but that has nothing to do with you. I am always here for you."

The boy's small soul fragment is very surprised to hear this, as the boy always thought that his father had left him. Now the soul fragment is willing to return to the boy, who is very happy about this.

I ask the small soul fragment that has returned what it needs. It wants the assurance from both parents that they will never leave him. I tell the boy that I am sure they will both give him this promise.

The parents are now asked to tell and reaffirm to their son that their separation had nothing to do with him but everything to do with them and that it is their issue to deal with, not his. They tell him that they love him. Even though they aren't together anymore, they will always be his loving parents.

I work with the boy on another two occasions after this, as well as several times with the mother individually to help her to get over the separation. Even the father comes to see me. Most of the boy's fear of falling asleep subsides soon after the first session and almost competely after the next two sessions.

In the final session, the boy draws his ball of soul energy again, and this time it is complete and bright. His parents are feeling better overall now too.

What Exactly Is Shamanism?

To understand shamanic soul retrieval, it helps to know a little about its background.

Shamanism exists everywhere

Shamanic practices have been passed down orally for forty-five thousand years and are among the oldest forms of healing in existence. They developed from the laws of nature and are practiced by all indigenous cultures attempting to live in balance with the natural world of which they consider themselves to be a part.

Whether Indian tribes in the Americas, African cultures such as the Dogon, Yoruba, and the San, or Australian Aborigines, Siberian and Mongolian indigenous peoples, or the Innuit, they all share similar practices and rituals. Thanks to these, they can connect with the so-called invisible world, the matrix or energy behind everything that is, to heal and live in harmony with existence.

In shamanism, people are taught that communicating with the source of all, the Divine, is a natural part of life. With the right techniques, everybody can learn to see and to communicate with the invisible world.

Shamanic practices are a pathway to what every one of us, all over the world, desires: love, health, meaning in life, freedom, and happiness in the here and now. They are a pathway to yourself, embedded in the world, nature, and the universe, connected with everything. There is no guru or priest who is the only bridge to God or who is the only one who can communicate with him. With the right techniques, everybody is capable of achieving this. This strengthens our confidence in the fact that all answers lie within ourselves and that we are connected to everything.

Shamanic techniques

Indigenous cultures begin initiation rituals for their children at an early age and continue to perform many ceremonies throughout the course of their lives. The methods are simple and easy to understand, and everybody can make use of them.

Among the most common techniques is inducing a trance state through drumming or other sounds, or through dance or adopting certain postures, communicating with power animals, the extraction or removal of the source of an illness, the phases of vision quests and rites of passage for all age groups, and ancestral and soul retrieval work.

It is not without reason that so many young people in today's modern culture dance to a pounding beat for days

and nights on end. They unknowingly enter a trance state in which they are closer to the Source, and have transcendental experiences.

In indigenous cultures, young people are prepared for adulthood through rites of passage in which they dance for hours in a trance. Later, as adults, they also take part in many such ceremonies, often in an ecstatic state. The North American Indian sun dance is one such example, when entire tribes gather to dance, sing, and play drums, entering a healing state of trance.

The methods used for initiation rites teach us how to recognize and feel the energy behind everything—the matrix, the invisible world, God. Shamanism views visible, physical life as a reflection of the invisible world. If you are balanced in your soul and in balance with the energy flowing through and behind all that exists, you also live in a harmonious and empowered state in reality.

Relativistic physics demonstrates that all matter is energy. It is this energy, invisible to the eye, that in shamanism is described as the so-called invisible world. We are in a permanent, reciprocal, two-way exchange with this invisible world; for example, in our dreams both at night and during the day.

The ancient shamans already understood this tens of thousands of years ago and used this knowledge to work within the matrix, this energy that is invisible to us but is nonetheless present and flowing through and behind all that exists. Everything in its smallest components consists of pure light and moves at the speed of light; for example, the light of the moon reaches the Earth in just one second.

In shamanic healing work, we work with this energy, this light, often covering huge distances through the matrix and the universe. As modern particle physics has shown, some atomic particles can travel even farther distances at even higher speeds.

It only takes a moment for me to leave the Earth. I enter a kind of wormhole and I'm flying through tunnels. Suddenly, very quickly and abruptly, I arrive. In a strange place in a faraway galaxy.

I see a bubble floating among the stars. Inside is a small child-soul, alone. It left its physical body when it was four years old. It had endured a great deal of violence in its family, too much to bear any longer. The soul had to get far away, to a distant galaxy, as far away in the universe as possible.

Today this soul's physical body is almost fifty years old and the man to whom the soul belongs has approached me, asking for his broken childhood to be healed. I am working with him in a trance. I ask his child-soul if it wants to now return, after forty-six years have passed. The soul is only too happy to do so and starts to weep.

All this takes place silently, with no communication in verbal terms. Together with my spirit guides, I bring the child-soul back through the wormhole and help it to reenter the soul and the man's body.

It is at this moment that tears spring to the man's eyes and he breathes out, his entire body relaxing.

Shamanism, supported by the World Health Organization (WHO)

What is common to all these ways in which to connect with the invisible world? They cause profound transformations in body and soul. You do not just study a philosophy using your mind but live it with your entire being. The results are real and physical. When you perform these techniques, you do not simply think about it, you actually have an energetic and physical impact. They change and influence the nervous and digestive systems, biochemistry, hormones, and the cerebral spinal fluid.

In a trance state the images you see are just visual translations of energy processes, but these processes actually produce hallucinogenic opiates and organic compounds in the brain. Take this example: If a tense, stressed person imagines they are taking a soothing, warm shower to relax and wash away their stress, the physical experience is exactly the same as if they really were taking a shower, except that they do not get wet. The nervous system reacts, the person relaxes.

In addition, in a trance state, our brain waves reach the range of 3–7 hertz, which corresponds to the pulse and "heartbeat" of the Earth. This allows us to tune in automatically to, and to be in harmony with, nature. Furthermore, both halves of the brain, the rational and the intuitive, connect during the process, leading to harmony and balance. One of the triggers for the depression so prevalent in today's world is precisely this separation of the right and left hemispheres of the brain.

The information in this book is based on Core Shamanism. This type of shamanic work is supported by the World Health Organization (WHO). It is valued by some as being just as effective in the treatment of psychosomatic problems as psychotherapy, and likewise in maintaining a healthy balance of the four aspects of being human: body, mind, emotions, soul.

However, shamanic work differs from the psychotherapeutic approach in one very important way—the inclusion of the spiritual, the mystery, and wonder of life. This is why, following a psychotherapy session, many people are able to understand the origin of their problems perfectly well, although everything remains the same on an energetic level in that they still feel lethargic, depressed, and desperate.

What's missing is the "energetic resolution" of old wounds, as Sandra Ingerman writes in her book *Soul Retrieval*[1]. As a psychotherapist herself, Sandra Ingerman began to effectively include shamanic work to support her clients in becoming truly happy and healthy, rather than just wishing for this outcome.

New Western shamanism

The phenomenon of similar knowledge existing universally in all shamanic cultures, no matter where in the world, was also observed by the American anthropologist Michael Harner.[1] He developed the Core Shamanism on which this book is based for people in the West by filtering out the different cultural customs such as the practice of chanting and the use of regalia. The West lost its own version of ancient shamanism during the Middle Ages.

It is a fact that in the Middle Ages, over the course of several hundred years, an estimated ten million people were murdered during witch hunts and the Inquisition. No other culture has quite so thoroughly destroyed its own natural connection to, and knowledge of, the Divine in such a short time as Western civilization. All that remains are the legends of ancient shamanic healing in the Nordic song collection known as the *Edda* and in the Celtic stories of the British Isles. Almost everything else was systematically wiped out.

Many women were killed, but the death toll also included men. Anyone possessing knowledge was a threat to the Church's hold on power, according to which only priests could communicate with the Divine. Certainly, there were some individual religious leaders with integrity and respect for humanity within the Church, but as a collective institution it felt threatened by anyone with knowledge of the healing powers of nature. The same was true of Western countries, which throughout history have been intent

upon conquering the lands of the indigenous nations of the world.

All those able to communicate with animals and nature, heal with herbs, or possessing knowledge of the stars, all those able to enter a trance and talk with the spirit world and the ancestors were condemned. Essentially, any person who lived with an open, free heart and mind was sentenced to death. And since shamanic techniques are passed on orally and through hands-on learning, the only way to destroy them was to murder those who practiced them.

Whereas in Europe shamanic techniques were wiped out entirely, in other parts of the world—among the indigenous cultures of the Americas, Africa, and Australia—some brave people took the knowledge underground, even though it often meant risking their lives.

It is only since 1978, for example, that Native American Indians and Hawaiians have been allowed to practice and live their spiritual beliefs and techniques, thanks to the American Indian Religious Freedom Act. Until then, they could be—and were—sent to prison. And in earlier times they could even be sentenced to death simply for building a sweatlodge or conducting ceremonies such as soul retrieval, huna, or shamanic healing work.

In the desire to find our roots again, we people of the West initially turned to the shamanic knowledge that these indigenous cultures still possessed intact. However, shamanic wisdom evolved from a universally applicable truth. It was developed over tens of thousands of years through trial and error, eventually becoming a common body of knowledge that helped people to survive. Western people who have reopened themselves to this universal and natural wisdom inherent in our cellular memory have also been able to reestablish the connection.

A new kind of shamanism has developed in Western countries, which goes by many different names, including matrix healing, hypnotherapy, quantum healing, and reiki. There is a resurgence of something that had been all but wiped out, even though it is actually indestructible, because it is the healing essence of everything.

Exercise

A journey into the soul world

Sit or lie down somewhere quiet where you won't be disturbed. The journey can be made in silence or supported by meditative music or shamanic drumming.

Now close your eyes and relax. Breathe in and out deeply. In your mind's eye, visualize a portal, a gateway into the invisible world, to the energy behind all life that is, into the matrix. Then take a deep breath and at your own pace step through the portal.

Notice your new surroundings. Without having any preconceived ideas as to which angel, being, or animal will come to you, say your name and call your spiritual guide or power animal to you.

You may not even see it but you sense it. Ask if it is your guide, if it is here to help you. Ask your companion guide for its gift, its messages for you, and ask any questions you may have. Ask also if you can do anything for your guide, if it needs anything from you.

Enjoy your encounter and charge yourself with the energy of your companion being or power animal.

Give thanks to your spiritual guide, take a deep breath and return through the portal into the present. Visualize how you step back into your body so that you arrive well-grounded in your everyday life once more. Take your time and open your eyes.

Why Do Soul Parts Leave?

Over time, due to painful and traumatic experiences, parts of our soul's energy leave us. They do not disappear, since energy can never disappear, but they travel to another place and hide or split off in our own energy field.

If, for instance, you grew up under harsh circumstances, had an accident, or were abused, the parts of your soul that are hurt will leave you because the pain is greater than you can bear at this time. This dissociation is at once a necessary survival mechanism and a means of self-protection.

Perhaps part of your soul is still with a former partner, someone you were never able to completely let go, or perhaps another part remains at the hospital where your appendix was removed in an operation as a child and is hiding in a dark corner.

If you have experienced severe emotional or sexual trauma, parts of your soul may have traveled to a distant part of the universe, as far away as possible, to hide in fear.

At the time and in that particular situation, there was no way for you to influence or process the painful condition.

This is why your soul plane took parts of your soul to places where they could no longer be hurt. It was the only option.

Microtrauma in everyday life

Events leading to fragmentation of the soul do not always need to be dramatic. They can also happen in everyday life, often through a recurring action. For example, when a child is teased by classmates at school over a long period of time, when somebody is bullied at work, a teacher repeatedly embarrasses an adolescent in front of the class, or when parents are always in a rush in the morning and are constantly pushing a child to hurry, an unpleasant daily walk or drive to work, constant arguments within the family or neighborhood, frequent noise pollution, when a young child or teenager has to move house with their parents and part of their soul stays behind with their friends at their previous home . . . the list is endless.

Our self-esteem and life force are impaired by the splitting off and dissociation of soul fragments.

Pregnancy and birth

Parts of the soul often fragment during problematic pregnancies and births. Many people do not even know what happened at their birth, whether it was easy or difficult, because they never discussed it with their mother.

Yet pregnancy and birth are our first impressions of life. They provide an initial pattern from which, like a needle in the groove of a record, our life carries on.

A person will go through life confidently if their mother's pregnancy and their birth went smoothly. They were able to come into the world through their own efforts—their first sense of achievement.

If the pregnancy and birth were difficult, however, this will be reflected in the person's life to come. If, for example, they had to be delivered with the help of forceps or a suction cup, they will often feel as though they are not making any progress in life or that they are being controlled by others. They lack essential life force.

Exercise

Relive your journey to life

Regardless of whether or not you know whether your birth was smooth or difficult, this exercise can be carried out if you would like to resolve whatever challenges may have occurred in the first phase of your life.

Find a quiet place in which to lie down and close your eyes. Relax and calm your breathing. In your mind's eye, visualize yourself as a small embryo in your mother's womb. Focus on how you felt there.

Now allow the months of pregnancy to pass and relive your birth. Notice everything that was difficult or problematic. Breathe in and out deeply so that what you recall can be released from your cellular memory through your breath.

Vizualize yourself again as a small embryo, but this time imagine the entire pregnancy and birth proceeding in the best possible way. As you do so, see or sense how all your soul fragments return to you. With a deep breath, draw them back into your soul. In this way, you bring yourself into the world anew once more.

Notice how you feel in comparison to before. Thank yourself, and take your time to come back to the here and now, and open your eyes once more.

Childhood

Soul fragments leave us particularly frequently during childhood because at a young age we are dependent on our parents. Certain behavioral patterns or actions of adults can be very painful for a small child. The child's soul often does not know how to help itself and has no choice but to flee, to leave the body and hide parts of itself in a safe place where it can no longer be harmed.

It is inevitable that even the most loving parents will hurt their child emotionally at some point. Adults have busy lives and have enough to do just to maintain a reasonable balance in daily life and sometimes overlook the fact that they might hurt their child psychologically with certain actions.

Nearly all of us are missing important soul parts from childhood. Experiencing these fragments finally being able to return to us, as adults and after decades, is very emotional.

A thirty-eight-year-old woman consulted me in my office. I have the impression that she is not really living, even though she would like to. For the soul retrieval, I travel to a dark place in the matrix, the invisible world, deep in the bowels of the Earth.

It is here in this dark place, cold and clammy, that we find two soul parts. One became dissociated from the soul of the woman when she was just two years old. I see her as a little girl. The other soul fragment is found beside her brother, who died at a young age. He is not able to move onward into the light because part of his sister is with him and he wants to look after her, yet nor can his sister live fully in the here and now because an important part of her accompanied her dead brother at the time of his death. Her ability to enjoy life went with him. And indeed the woman has only rarely felt happy since he passed away.

I tell the woman what is happening. She starts to cry. "I miss you so much. Why you and not me?" she asks the brother. I convey her brother's answer to her. "It was my fate, my path. It was not your fault. By living well and happily, you honor my destiny."

The woman is relieved. She says goodbye to her brother. As her soul fragment returns, so too finally does her zest for life, thirty-six years after his death.

Entangled lives and dependencies

Other people can also hold on to parts of our soul. This can occur frequently, for instance, with parents, family members, friends, partners, colleagues, teachers, and students.

It nearly always takes place unconsciously, passively, through a person's thoughts, and only very rarely through conscious action. Most of us have already taken parts of another person's soul or have had our own taken away. Someone who "steals" soul parts from others in this way is lacking in something in themselves. We often feel totally drained when soul fragments are taken from us.

People in supportive professions, such as doctors, nurses, caregivers, and therapists, but also celebrities, are particularly affected.

We steal soul fragments from others out of jealousy, because we want to maintain a relationship, or because we feel empty and as though something is missing. We are envious of another's vitality although we cannot use it. It will even harm us because then we are burdened with a soul part that does not belong to us.

A typical example is a former partner who does not want to let go, holding on to parts of our soul. They feel that they cannot live without us because they lack essential soul energy and vitality. Of course, the situation might also be reversed and we are the ones who do not want to let our partner go and therefore hold back soul parts from them.

The most vile example of soul theft and severe trauma must surely be the sexual abuse of babies, children, and teenagers, since at the root of the molesting lies the perpetrator's desire to take the victim's shining soul energy. We all know that babies and children are full of life and radiance. The abuser subconsciously wants to acquire this because they themselves are empty.

Since the majority of sex offenders were themselves once victims and have lost soul parts as a result of the abuse they suffered, they nearly always lack essential soul energy. This can sometimes continue for generations, but it stops exactly at the point that awareness and healing take place.

Repeated physical and emotional violence toward children is also part of this callous type of soul theft. Some adults repeatedly dominate children through words, actions, or violence. They make up for their own lack of vitality and strength by taking it from the child. "I am stronger than you" is, however, a false sense of self-worth.

Children cannot defend themselves against this behavior because they lack the physical strength, they want to be left alone, or because they are afraid that their parents might not love them anymore if they try to protect themselves.

This type of sexual, emotional, and physical abuse does not only affect children, of course, it also takes place among adults and even between societies and nations. War is the most extreme example, but the subconscious goal is always to take the other's life force and soul parts. Entire societies are affected. This power is misunderstood and has nothing to do with the personal power that we possess when we are at one with ourselves as complete, balanced souls. False power does not create wholeness in oneself.

That is why the healing and the completion of our own soul is always also a step toward peace on Earth, between countries and people.

Sometimes, however, we even give up parts of our soul voluntarily, either because we have given up on ourselves or are convinced another person needs our help. For instance, parents or partners who love "too much" or relationships in which codependency plays a role.

"Soul contracts" between people are usually unspoken agreements and obligations according to which each person should fill the other's lack. They can be created at birth, for example, through unhealthy entanglements and nonverbal agreements between parents and their children, or even date back to previous lives.

But in the end, soul parts that have been surrendered are only a burden for the other person. Almost everyone knows the feeling of carrying around something that does not belong to them, something that is too much.

To let go of soul parts that do not belong to you, it is often sufficient just to know that you have taken them in the first place—awareness of the fact is enough. Sometimes, however, focused healing work is also required. As soon as you release and return another's soul part, the energy between you becomes clear again. Relationships also often improve as a result.

The good thing is that when you are aware of the process of entangled dependence, nobody can steal or take possession of your soul parts on a permanent basis against your wishes. It is therefore clear that each and every one of us can learn something in the process. We can then peacefully let go of anything that isn't in accordance with ourselves.

Exercise

Becoming free in relationships

Close your eyes and center yourself. Be aware of the person who is still holding a part of your soul. This missing soul fragment might express itself, for example, as an old feeling of resentment or powerlessness.

When you are aware of the identity of the person concerned, imagine talking to them. Now repeat the following sentence four times, "I am not at your disposal anymore." This sentence can also be repeated when you do not know the identity of the person but nonetheless have a vague feeling that somebody has a part of your soul.

Now sense or visualize how your soul fragment returns to you. Take it by the hand and ask what qualities it has brought back to you, and what it needs from you so that it will stay with you.

Embrace this fragment and feel how it becomes one with your soul again. Enjoy this feeling of completeness.

Now be aware of any person whose soul part you are still holding. It might be expressed as a longing or pain.

Now release that part of the soul. Breathe it out with a powerful breath and say, "I now let you go in peace." Repeat this three more times.

Notice how you now feel. In doing so, sense and experience your new soul feeling. You are whole when you feel whole.

Trauma, coma, and death

Trauma can be caused by fateful experiences that shape and have an impact on a person for life, such as war, natural disaster, rape, abuse, violence, accidents, and serious operations for health issues.

A young girl has come to my office with her mother. She was born with a heart defect. Although still barely four years old, she has already undergone two major open-heart surgeries. She lifts up her shirt and shows me her scars. There are several, extending from below the stomach to the neck, along with scars on the neck and arms from the insertion of surgical tubes.

She still has several severe operations ahead of her. Her mother wants her daughter to have the stamina to be able to withstand everything that is still to come.

The little girl paints a picture of her soul for me. Like a partly eaten pizza, there is a large piece missing. And yet another large piece is missing in another part of her soul image.

I explain the soul retrieval ceremony to her. She nods, as if it were the most natural thing in the world. She stands up and stretches out her arms totally naturally as I light a smudging bowl containing sage. She visibly enjoys the experience as I bathe her body in the smoke.

During the soul retrieval ceremony, I tell her what I see and that a part of her soul has remained in the hospital. It hid in a room together with the soul fragments of many other children who had undergone operations there. She is happy that this part of her is returning once more.

I also tell her that I see she possesses a great deal of life force, otherwise she would not have been able to get through all this, and that she has an especially compassionate, loving heart and was once also a healer herself. She looks at me with wide eyes full of wisdom and dedication to life.

I accompanied this girl repeatedly in the years that followed and still do so today. She has now successfully undergone her serious and life-threatening operations. Although she will always have to take special care of her heart, she will be able to continue her life's journey with courage.

Coma patients barely have enough soul energy left to keep their bodies alive. They are unconscious, and often the soul does not know how to return to its body. In such cases, a soul retrieval ritual can help the injured or lost soul fragments to return, helping the patient either to regain consciousness or to let go and leave the body entirely.

A person can be too ill to die. Countless people vegetate in hospital in this condition for weeks, months, or even years. The soul might try to cross over into death, but it is not complete enough to die. Or there may be an unresolved issue in the life of a terminally ill person that is holding them back from making this transition. A soul retrieval can therefore lead to completeness and inner peace, so that an individual can then leave.

In the modern Western world, death is seen as a decisive cut-off point, the end of everything. In the shamanic world view, however, death is the transition to a new plane of existence. Letting go of the current life for something new often represents a profound healing.

There must be indescribable sublimity and grace in dying peacefully—consciously, with complete awareness and gratitude for having lived life to the full—and to be able to accept and embrace everything that has happened, including all experiences.

Past lives and collective themes

Many people have different kinds of memories from past lives—of wars, previous partners, living in other countries, being of a different gender . . . Whether they are personal experiences from past lives or collective memories of human history, I do not know.

But it does not really matter. What counts is that these memories and feelings exist, stored in our cells and in our cellular memory, and are passed down from generation to generation. These or similar events really did once take place.

I look down at my feet. I am wearing shoes that I do not own, at least not in my current lifetime. I am wearing a long, brown shirt and am simply sitting quietly in a forest, looking around. Next to me is a basket full of leaves, roots, and herbs. I know what they can be used for, what good they can do.

I am looking at a beautiful, large and ancient tree. It is communicating with me, telling me how I can help one particular woman to heal her illness.

I go to the woman's house and give her my herbal remedies. But as I do so, a man—her husband—runs up to me, shouting that this is devil's work. He starts hitting me. Other men and women from the town come and also beat me. I am kicked and stabbed to death by the mob. It is terrifying and horrific.

I suddenly realize why I sometimes have totally irrational fears about going public with my healing work, a real terror—because this work was once responsible for my death. I see the parts of my soul with the qualities of strength and courage that have not yet returned to me since this past life. I assure them that this time I am able to take good care of them, and they return to me.

My fear has now gone.

The symptoms of missing soul parts

The signs that you have lost part of your vital life force include extreme fatigue and feeling as though you have been cut off from life, as well as chronic illness, experiencing repeated accidents, and things falling apart in your life.

The feeling of "not being here," of somehow "not being complete" arises from parts of your soul energy having left your soul.

Many people try to compensate for this absent life force with food, alcohol, television, social media, work, or drugs. They frequently also try to make up for it with "recreational stress"—the desire to get out and do and experience ever more in their leisure time, restlessly chasing after life in search of fulfillment. But these are all futile attempts to fill the hole in the soul. Missing parts of the soul are nearly always the trigger for all kinds of addiction, but at the same time addiction is the search for what is missing.

A typical sign of soul fragments having gone astray is also the absence of the qualities associated with them. A clear example of this is an artist who knows they have the ability to paint, write, or make music, for example, but has a creative block; they are no longer able to be imaginative and creative no matter how hard they try. The reason is often that the soul part with the creative power has disappeared.

This principle, of course, likewise applies to other qualities. For example, someone who wants to start a new project but is not able to get it off the ground because the quality of initiative has split off and left the soul.

Missing soul parts are also the cause of most depression, one of the most common illnesses in the Western world today. Waking up in the morning and just wanting to go back to sleep, even though this planet is so beautiful, has almost become normal—more normal than being happy and feeling alive.

Exercise

Dismemberment

Take a look back at your life. When did you experience emotional, spiritual, or physical setbacks? What were the triggers?

Now close your eyes and take a few deep breaths. Imagine a portal, a gateway into your soul world, to the energy behind all life, to the matrix. Then take another deep breath and step through the portal.

Notice your new surroundings. Now call your helper beings. They may appear as angels or animals, but they may equally appear as feelings or manifestations of energy. Ask them for a "dismemberment" in which you are destroyed or taken apart and reassembled anew.

There's no cause for concern, nothing bad can happen to you. A dismemberment is an ancient shamanic method defined as death without dying or death-rebirth. On the one hand, tensions and old, outdated energy patterns dissolve, while on the other you experience your infinite and indestructible center which always exists and observes.

Dismemberment is a great cleansing ritual. Experience what wants to happen. A stone might fall on you, or you might explode from the inside, like a burst balloon, or an animal might devour you. Allow it to happen, observe and experience it—you are protected.

Then see how you reemerge, how you are cleansed, renewed, and reassembled. Enjoy this feeling of freshness, of being reborn.

When the process is complete and your journey is therefore at an end, give thanks to the invisible world. Take some deep breaths and return through the portal to the present. Imagine yourself stepping back into your body so that you arrive well-grounded in your everyday life. Open your eyes again in your own time.

Healing

Everyone may experience healing at some point in their lives, whether on a physical, mental, emotional, or spiritual level. Experiencing deep healing is a blessing of being human. It opens the heart and soul—to ourselves but also to our fellow human beings.

We all experience crucial points in our lives, times that simply hurt and seem impossible to resolve and heal because everything is just so painful. They include, for example, living through our parents' divorce as a child, surviving a catastrophe or living through a war, being betrayed and deserted by a partner, experiencing violence, losing a child or someone close to us, undergoing a severe illness or surgery.

All these experiences can cause soul fragments to leave and find their way to a safe place where nobody can harm them anymore.

Healing, however, is always possible. Walk through the dark night of the soul and come back into the light. Healing is part of human nature. We have all the necessary powers of self-healing within us.

Experience to the full what it means to live on Earth as a human being. Take a close look, leave out nothing. Living on Earth also involves being able to understand and manifest the light from the polar reality and suffering here. Those who have been hurt understand forgiveness, peace, and love in the depths of their being. Weep—because then you will be able to laugh. Experience the darkness so that you may recognize the light.

You too can now heal your deepest wounds with profound love and compassion toward yourself. You can become whole again.

Exercise

Self-healing

Sit down somewhere quiet. Close your eyes, calm your breathing, and relax. Focus on your heart. How does it feel?

Imagine that you see the small bud of a favorite flower in your heart; it is in a color that pleases you.

Now take your time to imagine this bud opening slowly. As you do so, with a deep breath, breathe out what you no longer need, even if you do not know exactly what that is—emotions, memories, dark spots. Every time you breathe in, the bud opens a little more, and every time you breathe out, you let go of the old so that there is room for the new in your heart.

See how the bud unfurls, opening out more and more, and how your heart is filled with beauty, love, and vitality. Enjoy how your heart and soul feel when the flower is fully open.

When you are ready, return to the present and open your eyes. Welcome to life!

How do soul parts come back to us?

Bringing back lost soul parts is a common practice in indigenous cultures. For example, if someone suffers an accident, they will initially be taken care of by a medicine man, similar to a Western doctor, but this will be followed by a vsit from a shaman to retrieve their lost soul fragments.

Modern psychology and psychotherapy also fulfill this function, but there is a limit as to the extent that they can be effective. Patients may understand their problems and issues and have them analyzed in depth, but their soul feels incomplete because its essence is still missing. Energetic healing has not taken place because the therapy they underwent only worked on the mind, not the soul.

This is why soul retrieval work is so effective.

Think about why you want to carry out a soul retrieval. What is wrong in your life? Which patterns of behavior would you like to stop? If you do not have a specific issue, you can ask to undertake a healing journey for your best possible development.

How do you retrieve your soul parts? You do not carry out the soul retrieval yourself. It is your helpers and guardian angels in the invisible world who heal you. They are your allies, your first point of contact. The guiding principle behind this is support from the spiritual world in the sense of the greater whole of which we are a part.

For a successful soul retrieval, it is important to build a good relationship with the healing forces of nature around you and to ask these forces to support you in your efforts. The most important thing that you can offer them is your trust—trust in these higher forces and powers of the universe that originally allowed you to enter this world as a soul in a physical body. That we human beings even exist is a miracle that we can never understand, a mystery that we can never comprehend.

With this kind of healing work, you are encouraged not to analyze what is taking place intellectually, you can do that later. If something in the process is unclear, you can always ask your helpers in the invisible world.

For the sake of simplicity, I refer to your helpers as guardian angels. However, they might appear in a totally different guise, such as light phenomena, animals, or even figuratively, as painted images. If you are tactile by nature, they might simply manifest as a sense that something is here to help you. The ways in which your helper beings from the energetic world reveal themselves are your mind's visual and emotional "translations" of energies in the universe that you can perceive in this way.

Soul fragments nearly always return voluntarily and are relieved to find you again. Sometimes they are afraid of returning, fearing that something painful could happen to them again. In this case, it is necessary to promise them that you, as an adult, will take good care of them.

It is generally better to perform a soul retrieval during the day as it is easy to fall asleep during the ritual. The work is very intense, even if it may appear gentle, and the person undergoing the ritual frequently feels very hungry afterward because so much energy has been moved.

For a successful outcome, it is also advisable not to drink alcohol or to take any other intoxicating substances for twenty-four hours before or after the ritual.

Exercise

Soul retrieval

Choose a place in which you can sit or lie down and remain undisturbed. Close your eyes, relax, and take some deep breaths in and out.

Now, in your mind's eye, visualize a portal, a gateway into the invisible world, to the energy behind all life that is, into the matrix. Then take a deep breath and pass through the gate at your own pace. Take note of your new surroundings.

Say your name and call your guardian angel. When you sense that your angel has come to you, ask it to guide you to your lost soul fragment. Alternatively, your guardian angel might also bring your soul fragment directly to you.

When you encounter one of your soul fragments, ask it to confirm that it does belong to you. Ask it which of your qualities or characteristic traits it has, and when and why it left you. Take your time until you have all the answers you need.

Now ask this soul fragment what it requires so that it may return and remain with you. Again, allow yourself all the time that you need. Afterward, take your soul fragment by the hand and embrace it so that you become one and are whole once more.

This exercise can be carried out as often as you like. You are whole when you feel whole.

Time for action

After a soul retrieval, you are more present, more in your body, because your essence, your soul, is closer to completeness. The changes are often subtle; you might notice that you feel better and more at ease overall.

The effect is usually noticeable more or less immediately, but generally unfolding within fourteen days and continuing until it is felt to the fullest extent. Sometimes entire months can go by, or it might not even be until years later that you suddenly have an insight into an image received during a soul retrieval that you might not have fully understood at the time. It is as if the pieces of your personal puzzle are coming together, which indeed they are. You become whole again.

Sometimes the painful feelings and memories that originally prompted the soul fragments to leave your body return with the retrieved soul parts. Old feelings of grief, fear, or anger can resurface, similar to an initial aggravation in homeopathy, but this does not have to be the case.

In such situations, the best thing to do is to treat it like a cold, which generally lasts around seven to ten days regardless of whether or not you take any medicine. During this time, you look after yourself and take it easy until the cold is over. It is no big deal. The same applies to painful memories or physical symptoms that can return with your soul parts. These intense feelings usually last no more than a few days, sometimes perhaps up to two weeks. Notice them and feel them, but do not try to do anything about them. As with a cold, they will pass, they are nothing but a memory of events that are now over. Look forward after seeing and honoring the past.

And just as catching a cold eventually strengthens your immune system, you feel cleansed after such a process, and often even reborn.

Essentially, any technique that helps people to solve their problems and feel better will bring back lost soul parts. A massage, pampering yourself, taking a vacation, and so on, can all be exactly what your soul fragments need to finally return to you. A shamanic soul retrieval may not always be required.

As I have found with both myself and my clients, once you have understood the principle of soul retrieval work and the complete soul as a luminous sphere, the healing process is always quicker and easier. You retain your vital energy within yourself because you know exactly what makes it leave and therefore take better care of yourself.

Maintaining Vitality: Care of the Soul

Integrating soul parts

Once soul fragments have returned, it makes sense to pay attention to them so that they remain with you. Your soul fragment needs a few days of rest and recovery, just as your body does after a long, weary journey. You take care of yourself so that all will be well.

Soul fragments can be successfully reintegrated by making a trance journey to learn more about them. Ask your soul fragment the questions in the exercise on the following page while taking a walk outside in nature and thank it.

Exercise

Soul part integration

Find a quiet place in which you can stand undisturbed. Take a few deep breaths and settle and center yourself. Then call the part of your soul that recently returned to you and visualize it standing directly in front of you.

Now take a big step and take the place of your soul fragment. How does it feel?

Ask why it initially left you and what skills, qualities, and talents went with it but have now returned to you.

Do you need to make any changes in your life so that your soul fragment will feel comfortable and remain with you? Would it like a particular ritual or action to be carried out that shows your appreciation in order for it to stay?

Sense and enjoy its vitality. Let it tell you in its own way how it feels at the moment, what it would like to do and experience right now. Perhaps it would like to jump around and dance a little. Remain in your soul part's place for as long as you like. Ask it anything you want to know.

Imagine taking your soul part by the hand and embrace it. To do this, grasp your right hand with your left and in this way you embrace yourself. Merge with your soul fragment, breathing deeply as you do so and enjoy the bonding and unity. Finally, together with your soul part, take a step back into your life, back into the here and now.

The characteristics of a healthy and complete soul

Being passionate and excited about something gives us purpose, providing incentive to get up in the morning. We know what we have to do and we feel good about it. It makes us feel alive and full of vitality.

Enthusiasm or a passion for something takes many forms: the excitement of romantic love, the commitment toward a just cause, the eagerness to realize a vision, or the desire to do something that you simply enjoy, such as playing music, traveling, sport, painting, or reading. Enthusiasm means having passion and a zest and love of life. What inspires you leads you to your life's purpose.

You love your life's purpose and work. It may represent a great challenge, but it is one that you know you must face. It is what allows you to grow within and your soul to shine. The only person who knows the calling or mission that inspires you is you yourself, so be honest. What is your true heart's desire? Do not be afraid of your passion because it will stimulate, drive, and strengthen you naturally. Listen to your dreams. They will bring great passion and enthusiasm into your life.

To live—that's exactly what life is for! It is a gift from heaven for you, something with magical possibilities and surprises. The universe is friendly and will support you when you open yourself up to it.

Enter this garden of delight. Open your heart in anticipation, expecting enchanting experiences, everywhere and always. Surprises are life's wonderful gifts. Cherish these experiences. Laugh wth joy and approach life with humor. Enjoy being alive.

You are whole when you feel whole

The figure shown on this page is fulfilled and surrounded by shining stars. The figure recognizes itself as part of the Divine, as a spark of the first light. It receives and holds the vibrant light—its life energy. It smiles, feeling its connection to the Divine world from which it receives protection and guidance.

You yourself are this figure. You are powerful, a child of God, full of self-confidence and vitality. You are whole, in the here and now, connected to the mystery and wonder of life, the magical and the mystical. That you exist here on Earth is a miracle.

The invisible world opens up to everyone who truly seeks healing, wholeness, and truth. You enjoy your healthy and complete soul, or will soon do so, no matter at what stage of life you are currently.

Exercise

A journey into your inner garden

Lie down in a quiet place. Take some deep breaths in and out and slowly close your eyes.

Now imagine your inner garden. This is your inner home, your place of power. It can be exactly as you like, such as a tropical rainforest, somewhere high up in the mountains, or your own garden. You can redesign your inner garden, which you see within yourself, at any time, to suit your needs and to make you feel comfortable and at home.

Now in your mind's eye, enter your inner garden. Visualize how you cleanse yourself there, perhaps in a lake or ocean, in a river or under a waterfall. Then lie down, enjoy the atmosphere, and relax. Notice what surrounds you in your inner garden. What plants or animals do you see? See how you regenerate.

When you are ready, return and slowly open your eyes once more. You can visit your inner garden at any time and as often as you like.

Health from the Shamanic Perspective

In shamanism there is no distinction between physical and energetic health. All aspects of a person are taken into account to make a diagnosis because all levels are connected.

The seven chakras, the human energy centres, represent the many aspects that make up a healthy person. The root chakra, between the perineum and genitals, is conerned with the physical, as well as with security, prosperity, and grounding. The second chakra, the sacral chakra, located just below the navel, is about sexual energy and emotions. The solar plexus chakra concerns joy, self-confidence, and willpower, while the heart chakra encompasses love, heart intelligence, and compassion. The throat chakra deals with creativity and communication, the third eye chakra focuses on intuition, spirit, concentration, and vision. And finally the crown chakra, located on the top of the skull, is about spirituality and the soul.

Take your time to consider all these aspects of your life. Think about in which areas you can take better care of yourself for the sake of your health so that you can become the being of light that you are destined to be. It is a wonderful feeling to be a complete and healthy human being, and to bring light to the Earth.

Illness: too little or too much

From the shamanic perspective, when somebody is ill it can affect them on every level: mind and body, emotions and soul, as well as the chakras. The origin of an illness is nearly always some form of soul loss and so has an energetic, spiritual cause.

There are two possibilities: either a lack or an excess. The loss of fragments of the soul creates a lack, a deficiency, and a person is weakened. However, this can, in turn, create an excess, as space is created within a person for "intruders," which leads to an excess of something. Despite this, a deficiency does not necessarily lead to a surplus.

Intruders and possessions

You might be familiar with the feeling that something is weighing heavily on your stomach or is sitting on the back of your neck. You may have also had the feeling that someone or something has taken possession of you, as if something is clinging to you or has even crawled inside you unseen.

In shamanic healing work, such energetic phenomena are known as intruders, foreign energies, or possessions. They are not evil, but are simply in the wrong place—namely in or with you.

Imagine it this way: When a house has a hole in its exterior wall, intruders such as insects and mice can enter through it. These creatures are not bad, they simply want to find their way into the warmth and where there might also be something to eat.

So when you have an energetic hole on some level—and this happens to everyone at some point, especially when they are tired or strained, out of balance or simply lacking a soul part—then all kinds of foreign energies can also find their way to you through this hole. They generally arise from thoughts and feelings.

Here's an example: You take the subway. A woman sitting behind you is angry about someone. Some of her thoughts, which have nothing to do with you per se, can enter you through your energetic hole.

These intruders can, of course, enter you more easily and intensively if a person with negative thoughts is someone who knows you well and is perhaps also consciously thinking about you. Foreign energies can then arrive from anywhere and enter you. This occurs through the so-called all-knowing, morphogenetic field—also studied in quantum physics—in which everything is always connected with everything else.

When energies, which in shamanism are described as entire soul entities or soul parts, enter someone, they are termed possessions and "occupations."

An example: A person has died, but does not know that they can move on to the great light of the Source, perhaps because they never thought about death. Therefore, they instinctively seek another light and find refuge there. Such a light can be the soul of a living person to which the wandering soul part clings when this person has an energetic hole.

Possessions can, however, also be other entities that exist in the universe and between heaven and Earth. They can, but do not necessarily, lead to severe personality disorders and the development of multiple personalities.

All this may at first glance appear very disturbing. However, it is totally natural—it occurs simply because there are so many living beings and energy forms on Earth and in the universe. And with the appropriate methods, a person can easily cleanse themselves again, and of course also reseal the energetic hole in the wall of their "house."

The best form of protection is to be in your center, in other words to be balanced, with a complete core and all parts of your soul. It is then only rarely that something can happen to you. It is neglecting the body, emotions, mind, and soul that makes people ill. Only the clearing, cleansing, and completion of your subtle body can make and keep you healthy.

Many people have high expectations of shamanic healing methods, frequently because they have already consulted countless conventional medical practitioners. And indeed, two-thirds of all known illnesses cannot be fully explained or healed by modern medicine, which merely alleviates the symptoms.

The causes often originate in a totally different location from where the symptoms appear. For instance, stomach problems may be related to the heart because parts of the soul have been lost through heartbreak. Foreign energies were therefore able to enter the body, such as through the stomach and intestines, from where the body tried to expel them again, triggering chronic stomach and intestinal complaints. But the root of the problem always lies in the loss of fragments of the soul, in lack or deficit.

In shamanism, miraculous healings are rare. Instead, they can nearly always be attributed to ancient methods, such as those described in this book, and are well-founded. It makes sense therefore to complement conventional with alternative medicine, thus making use of the best of them both.

Exercise

Cleansing foreign energies

Lie down in a quiet place. Close your eyes and take a few deep breaths in and out.

Imagine you are lying in a tunnel of radiant light in a color that is pleasing to you. Now, in your mind's eye, begin scanning yourself from your head to your toes. Where do you see dark spots, or perceive unpleasant feelings or foreign energies?

They often appear as nails or splinters, even as insects or worms. If you are tactile by nature, you may also feel them. But notice also where you feel healthy, radiant, and vibrant. Take your time and scan your whole body carefully.

Now, with deep breaths in and out, vizualize how the light in the tunnel streams through you and cleanses you, removing all intruders, possessions, dark spots, and unpleasant feelings.

Breathe out everything that you no longer need, even if you are not sure exactly what this is, and breathe in new strength, energy, and vitality. Remain bathed in this light until you feel completely cleansed.

To be totally sure that you are completely free and cleansed of all foreign energies, you can now ask the invisible world for support. Ask your guardian angel to remove everything that does not belong to you, everything that hurts or could harm you. Breathe in and out a few times deeply.

Allow this cleansing to take place through your guardian angel and give thanks.

Notice how you feel in comparison with before. Imagine how the tunnel of light surrounding you becomes a sphere. This ball of light will seal all the energetic holes through which intruders were able to enter and make you whole again. It is just the right size to make you feel safe and secure. Vizualize the light in a transluscent color that makes you feel good.

This—your—ball of light protects your life force. It keeps your four levels of being human—body, soul, mind, and emotions—safe and secure so that nothing is lost and nothing from outside can intrude and throw you off balance.

Be fully aware of the ball of light that cocoons you. Feel how it protects and preserves you. If you wish, from now on it can always be by your side. Enjoy its comfort for as long as you like, and when you are ready, return to the present and open your eyes again.

You are powerful, a child of God, healthy and full of vitality!

Soul Retrieval for the Earth

In the shamanic world view, everything has a soul, not only humans. Stones, trees, animals, and even the Earth—everything contains a unique consciousness. The realm of stones and minerals, for example, is considered the skeleton, the framework of Mother Earth. Stones and minerals are the oldest substances on the planet and contain great wisdom and solar power. The realms of plants, animals, and humankind also each have their own special qualitites.

We too belong to nature. Just as our bodies are crisscrossed by a network of blood vessels and are made up of cells, so the rivers and veins of minerals are the blood vessels of the Earth and the people its cells. The Earth is so beautiful and magnificent, it provides us with food, clothing, and a place to live. We are part of the Earth. When we care for it, we also care for ourselves. It is our home.

Think about your actions in terms of sustainability and benefit to the Earth. Do you ever consider the results of your daily actions on the next seven generations? Are you mindful? How can you care for the Earth responsibly?

Soul loss in nature and the Earth

It is not only humans who find parts of their souls to be lacking, this also applies to certain areas of the Earth. These are usually places where war has raged or the land has been ravaged by so much pollution and so many of the Earth's resources have been plundered that you feel the need to get away as quickly as possible because they feel so empty, haunting, and painful. You can sense the harm that has been done to nature, to the animals, and the people there.

In the teachings of the Hopi people, conditions such as these even have their own specific name, **koyaanisqatsi**, meaning a life out of balance, decay, and corruption—in short, a way of life that calls for change.

Director Godfrey Reggio named his award-winning, cult 1982 film after this Hopi word. In it the filmmaker shows images of the hectic Western world set to music by Philip Glass. His focus is on accentuating the ever-increasing speed and flow of information in our time: millions of cars on highways, thousands of people rushing through city streets, the city lit up by artificial lighting. Striking images depict the haste and soullessness of our age, as well as the pointlessness behind it.

A world out of balance. People out of balance. People with starved souls. People chasing something, without really knowing what that something actually is. It is their soul for which they are searching, and that of parts of the Earth.

The healing and completion of one's own soul is also always a step toward healing and peace in this world, for the Earth, and between countries and peoples. Finding peace and being at peace with oneself is a big challenge. Both the past and the current state of our "Blue Planet" demonstrate this. We live in a time of great change.

Earth's energy must be renewed, new ideas need space, the body and soul need new challenges. The future has become the present. Now all dreams other than those built on prejudice have the chance to become reality. What is important remains. What is unimportant will vanish.

We are all needed. We are here for a reason. Everyone living on Earth right now has an important purpose. Remember to look after your planet, whatever your contribution may be. You will do this naturally when you see yourself as part of the Earth.

May peace and health be within you and on Earth.

Exercise

Soul retrieval for the Earth

Perform a soul retrieval for an area of land. This could be an area of forest that appears soulless, a desolate area in your city or even your own garden.

Visit the location concerned and ask it if it would like you to conduct a soul retrieval. If you sense a positive answer, sit down in the location, close your eyes, relax, and take several deep breaths in and out.

Now, in your mind's eye, visualize a portal, a gateway into the invisible world, to the energy behind all life that is, into the matrix. Then take a deep breath and, in your own time, step through the portal. Notice your new surroundings.

Say your name and call your guardian angel to you. When your angel has appeared and you can perceive it, ask it to guide you to the lost soul fragment of the location. The angel might even bring this soul part to you.

When you encounter the soul fragment, ask it to confirm that it is the appropriate piece, what qualities it contains, and when and why it originally left. Take your time until you have learned everything.

Now ask the fragment what it needs so that it may return to, and remain in, the location. Again, take your time. Then do whatever the location has requested of you. For example, perform a small ceremony or say a prayer. Or perhaps the request is something else, such as planting some flowers in the location or cleaning up any trash. Listen to what the Earth is telling you.

May the healing that you perform for the Earth also be beneficial for you and all beings, in the spirit of the greater whole.

Acknowledgements

I would like to thank my parents, for without them I would not be on Earth. I would like to thank them for their love. I see that they have given me many good things for my path. I would also like to thank them for allowing me to embark upon my path as a healer, despite things that were not ideal in my family of origin.

I thank my many teachers from whom I was able to learn. For the knowledge in this book, I would especially like to thank Hermann Strohmeier, Sandra Ingerman, and Sun Bear, my teachers for shamanic soul retrieval, as well as my guides and aides in the spiritual world.

Thanks to my publishers, Heidi and Markus Schirner, for their faith in me and their support in bringing my work to the world. I would also like to say thank you to my editor Rudolf Garski, with whom I have been able to realize several projects. His understanding of communication and language has helped me to express even better and more clearly what I want to convey with my writing.

Bibliography

Sandra Ingerman: *Soul Retrieval: Mending the Fragmented Self*; HarperOne, 2006

Michael Harner: *The Way of the Shaman*; HarperOne, 1990

Sun Bear: *The Path of Power*; Simon & Schuster, 1995

Lisa Biritz: *Dolphins, Whales and Star Beings – A Journey Home*; United P.C., 2013

Lisa Biritz: *Soul Medicine: Inner Wholeness through Shamanic Soul Retrieval*; Oracle Cards Schirner, 2014

Picture credits

Floral ornaments: Silja Bernspitz, Schirner
Page 45: Lisa Biritz and wenani/shutterstock.com
Page 103: Lisa Biritz and Hilda Protschka

All others: shutterstock.com
Page 2: Oksana Shufrych; p. 6: SergeBertasiusPhotography; p. 14: Peshkova; p. 16 Happy Stock Photo; p. 19, 23: happykanppy; p. 25: Irina Bort; p. 29: T.Vyc; p. 32: Pikoso.kz; p. 34: Serg64; p. 36: Bruce Rolff; p. 39: wenani; p. 41: Fer Gregory; p. 48: Katrina Elena; p. 50 : Olesia Bilkei; p. 52: FXQuadro; p. 56: Przemek Klos; p. 61: perfectlab; p. 63: GoodFocused; p. 64: Mila Supinskaya Glashchenko; p. 66: Maxim van Asseldonk; p. 68: Pakhnyushchy; p. 71: Kira Volkov; p. 72, 74: Katerina Planina; p. 76: carlosobriganti; p. 80: Cranach; p. 83: Dormitria; p. 86: Pavel L Photo and Video; p. 90: Subbotina Anna; p. 92: Luboffke; p. 95: Benjavisa Ruangvaree Art; p. 98: M.Aurelius; p. 105: picExp; p. 108: Sunny studio

About the author

© Diana Sayegh

Lisa Biritz, author of *Shamanic Star Wisdom Oracle*, learned shamanic practices from the work of Sandra Ingerman (Core Shamanism) and Sun Bear. She leads seminars and organizes unique experiences, such as encounters with wild dolphins and whales. Born in the Netherlands and the mother of twins, Lisa now divides her time between Hawaii and Vienna.

Further information:
www.LisaRainbow.com